Pirates

with Jake Rattlebones

Philip Steele

KINGFISHER

Kingfisher Publications Plc
New Penderel House
283–288 High Holborn
London WC1V 7HZ
www.kingfisherpub.com

First published by Kingfisher Publications Plc 2007
2 4 6 8 10 9 7 5 3 1

1TR/0107/SNPEXCEL/SCHOY(SCHOY)/157MA/C

A CIP catalogue record for this book is available from the British Library.

ISBN 978 07534 1398 2

Senior editor: Catherine Brereton
Senior designers: Peter Clayman, Carol Ann Davis
Consultant: Richard Platt
Picture research manager: Cee Weston-Baker
Picture researcher: Rachael Swann
DTP co-ordinator: Catherine Hibbert
Senior production controller: Lindsey Scott

Printed in China

Contents

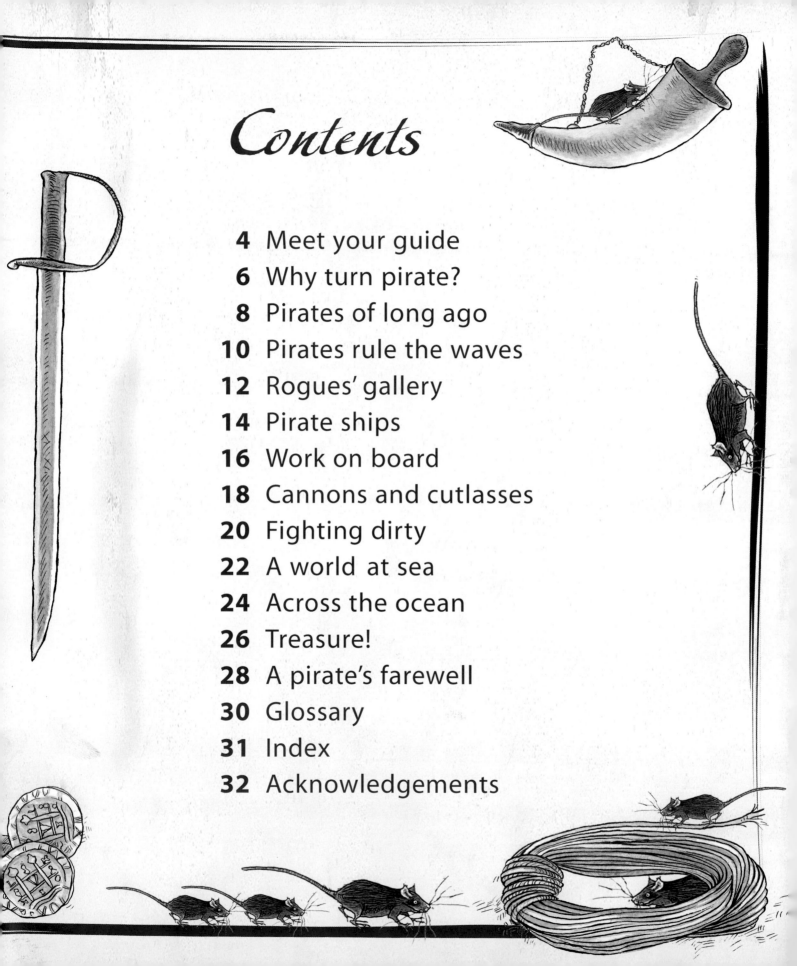

Meet your guide

My name is Jake Rogers, but my shipmates call me 'Rattlebones'. We pirates like scary names. Yes, I am a pirate, one of those villainous wretches who attack ships at sea, or towns and villages along the coast. We carry off whatever treasure takes our fancy. Sometimes we steal the whole ship and its cargo too!

"Jake Rattlebones at your service, with a dagger and a smile!"

modern-day pirates in Indonesia

I'm speaking to you from the year 1720, when bold pirates sail all the Seven Seas. There have always been pirates – and I bet there always will be.

Why turn pirate?

What made an honest sailor take up a life of piracy? Some lads ran away from ships where the captain gave them a hard time. Some had escaped from jail or slavery. Pirates could be cruel people – greedy, violent and even murderous. Some, like me, started as poor boys who dreamed of riches and adventure.

Could girls be pirates?

The real villains were the wealthy merchants who funded pirate trips. They got rich with none of the danger!

"I've met the captain and I want to join his pirate crew, so I'm signing my name here."

In the back room of many dockside taverns there was usually someone signing up to join a pirate crew. 'Going on the account', pirates called it.

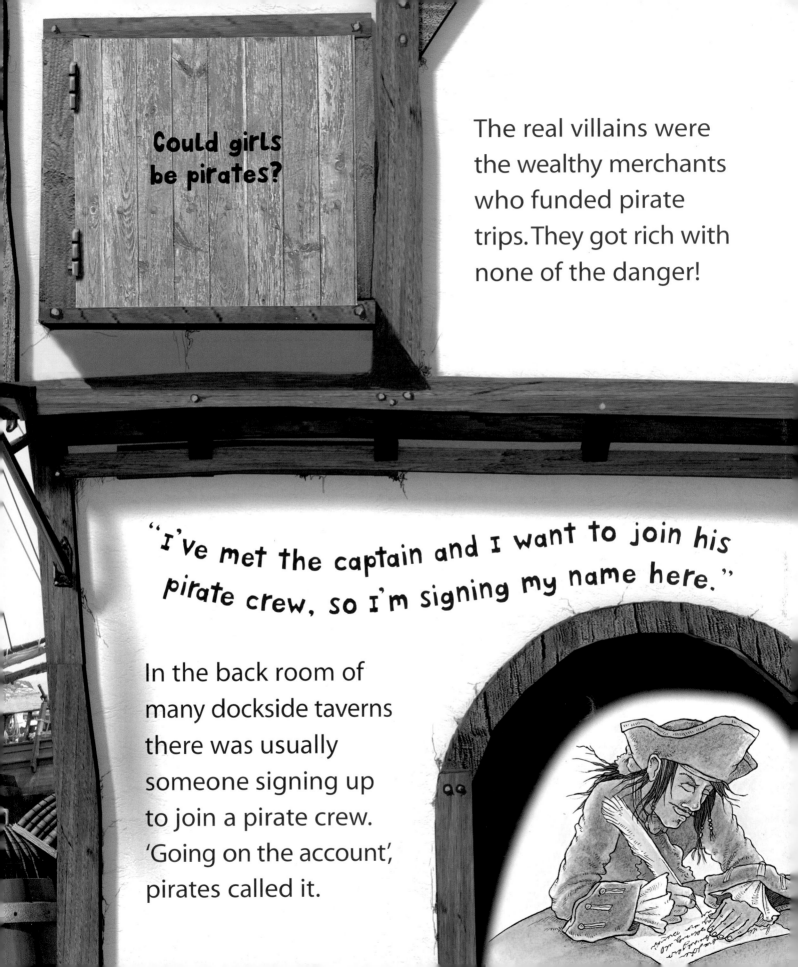

Pirates of long ago

Awise old captain once told me that pirates have been around for thousands of years. Pirates robbed ancient Greek merchant ships from around the 10th century BCE, and Roman ones from the first century BCE.

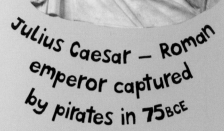

Julius Caesar – Roman emperor captured by pirates in 75BCE

pirates attacking a Roman merchant ship (75BCE)

In the 10th century CE, the Vikings sailed from northern lands in their longships. They fought with swords and battle-axes. Sea-wolves, people named them. Later, fierce pirates, called corsairs, infested the coasts and islands of the Mediterranean Sea.

Viking treasure (10th-13th century CE)

"Vikings attacked coastal towns, killing people and stealing treasures."

Khayr ad-Din (1470-1546), a corsair

a ship of Viking sea-wolves (900s CE)

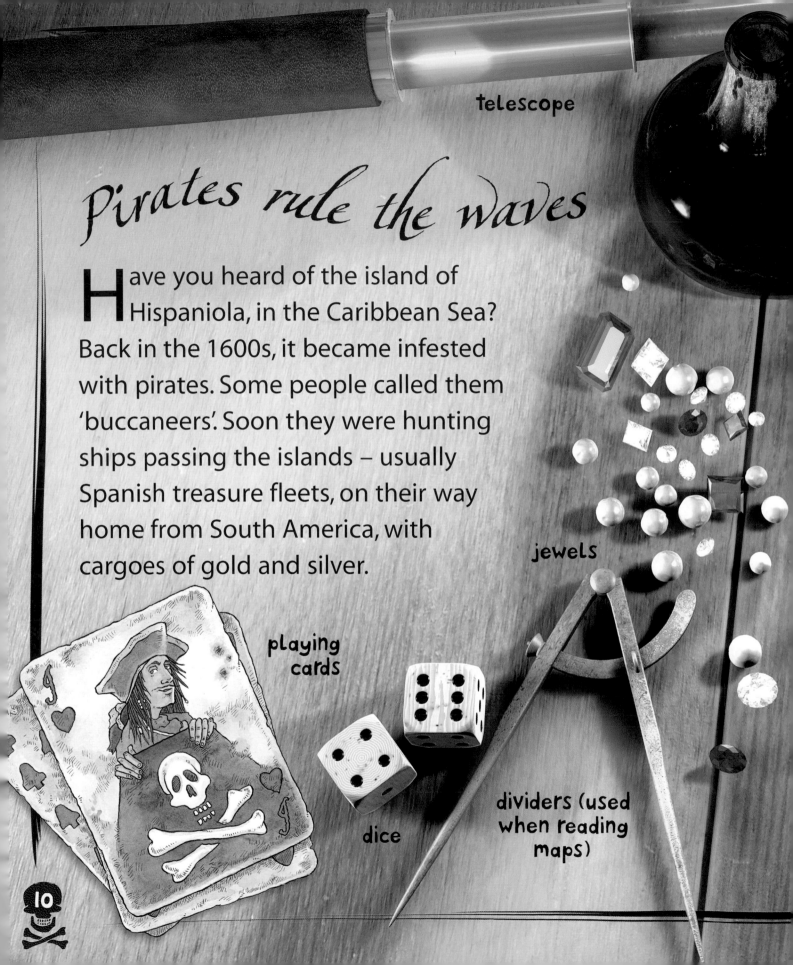

telescope

Pirates rule the waves

Have you heard of the island of Hispaniola, in the Caribbean Sea? Back in the 1600s, it became infested with pirates. Some people called them 'buccaneers'. Soon they were hunting ships passing the islands – usually Spanish treasure fleets, on their way home from South America, with cargoes of gold and silver.

jewels

playing cards

dice

dividers (used when reading maps)

tankard

bottle

The 1600s were the start of a new age of piracy. In my own day I have followed the 'Pirate Round', a long and risky voyage.

compass

Map of the Pirate Round

Some pirate captains set up their own private kingdoms in Madagascar, the main base on the Pirate Round.

gold coins

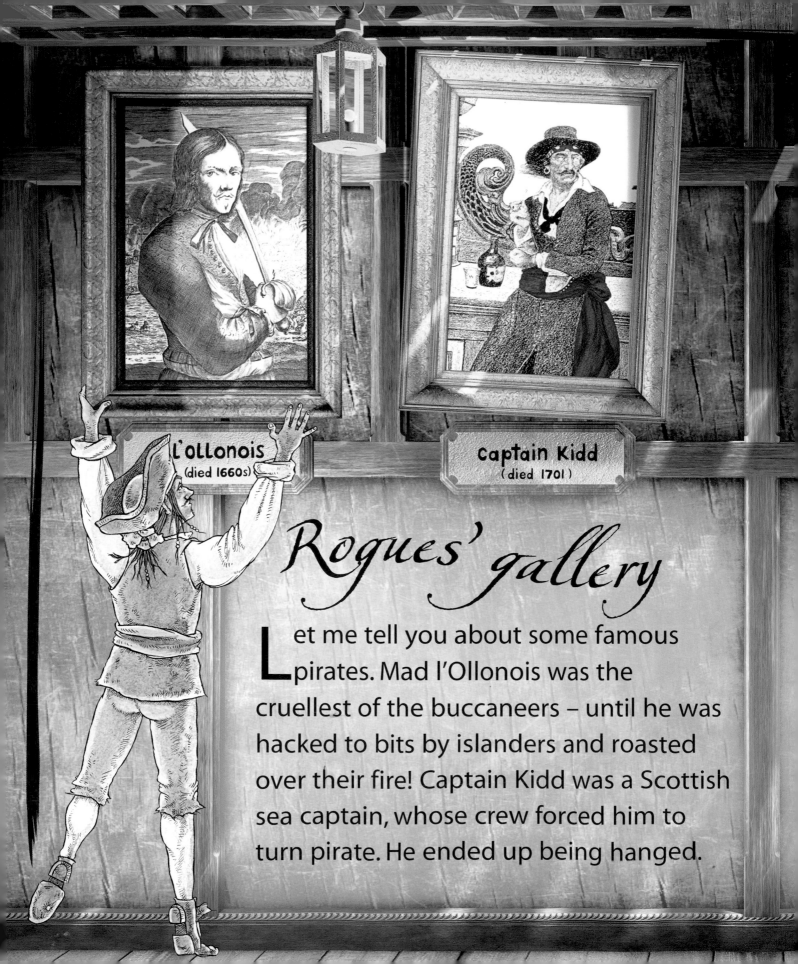

L'Ollonois
(died 1660s)

Captain Kidd
(died 1701)

Rogues' gallery

Let me tell you about some famous pirates. Mad l'Ollonois was the cruellest of the buccaneers – until he was hacked to bits by islanders and roasted over their fire! Captain Kidd was a Scottish sea captain, whose crew forced him to turn pirate. He ended up being hanged.

Blackbeard
(died 1718)

Bart Roberts
(died 1722)

Old Edward Teach, or Blackbeard, tied smoking fuses in his long, plaited hair to terrify his victims. Bart Roberts was the most daring of them all. They say he captured over 400 ships in just three years.

Pirate flags

Each pirate captain had his own flag, meant to strike fear into sailors' hearts and warn them not to fight. Here are some of the most gruesome designs...

Pirate ships

Pirates sail whatever ships they can steal or capture in battle. Small, fast vessels are the best because they can move easily at sea – good for chasing, or escaping up a shallow creek if they need to hide. The sloop was always my ideal ship. But if pirates can catch a big ship with lots of guns, they do!

SLOOP

Pirate ships through the ages

Greek pirate ship
580 BCE

Spanish galleon
1580

Barbary corsair
1660

English privateer
1720

Chinese junk
1845

Big ships take a lot of looking after, though – mending leaks, scraping off barnacles and stitching canvas.

"We like to capture ships that we can put to good use. We sink the rest!"

Work on board

Pirates share all the hard work on board ship. They scrub the decks and keep watch. They go aloft (climb the rigging) to mend and adjust sails, even in stormy weather. They must row out to islands they pass, to fill barrels of fresh water. Drinking seawater makes you sick!

keeping watch

What was pirate food like?

going aloft

navigating

Pirates won't take nonsense from anyone – captain or cabin boy. If any of the crew let each other down, they will be sorry they were born.

steering

scrubbing the deck

"why is it always me who gets the nasty jobs on board – such as catching rats?"

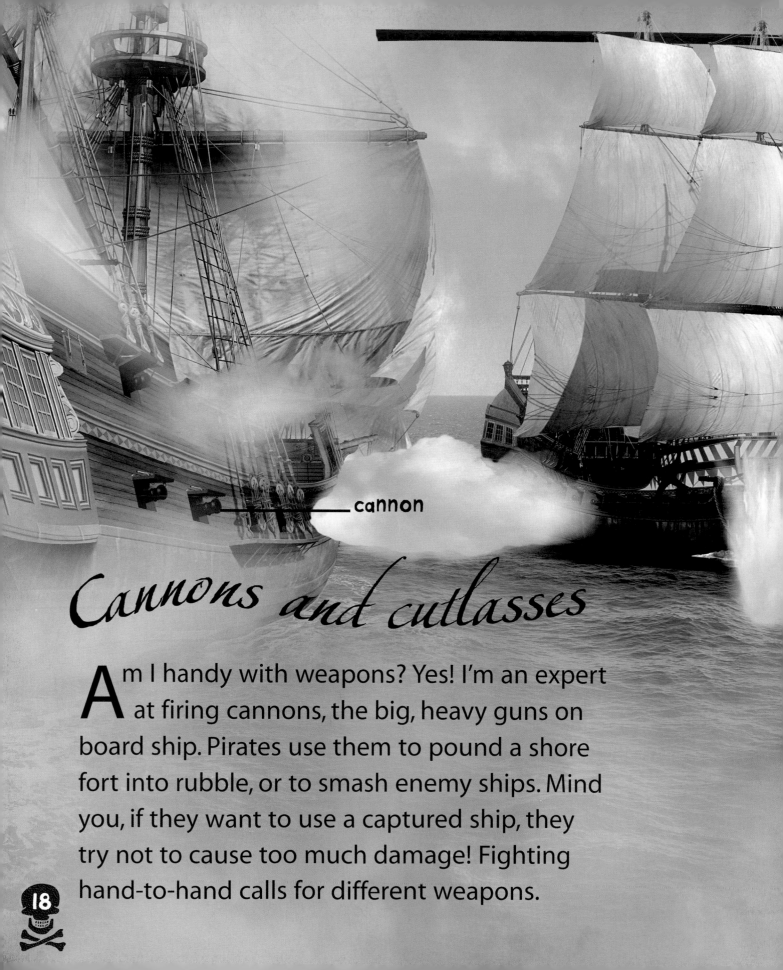

cannon

Cannons and cutlasses

Am I handy with weapons? Yes! I'm an expert at firing cannons, the big, heavy guns on board ship. Pirates use them to pound a shore fort into rubble, or to smash enemy ships. Mind you, if they want to use a captured ship, they try not to cause too much damage! Fighting hand-to-hand calls for different weapons.

cutlass and scabbard
(1770s)

pistol (1780s)

"Don't go striking a spark near the gunpowder store, or you will blow up the whole ship and crew!"

The sharp cutlasses sailors use are deadly in battle. I can fight with a sword or an axe, a pistol, a musket or a dagger – or even a broken table leg if I have to.

How to fire a cannon

1. Ram the gunpowder down the barrel, then load the shot (the cannonball).

2. Haul the heavy cannon to the gun port with ropes. Then light the fuse…

3. …BANG! The explosion sends the cannonball flying out. Ropes hold the cannon as it rolls back.

Fighting dirty

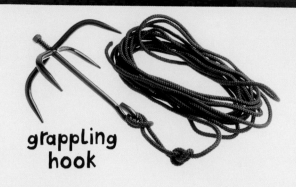

grappling
hook

Do you know what is the best weapon a pirate captain has? His cunning. The first trick is to give the enemy a false sense of security. Keep all weapons out of sight. Fly 'false colours' and pretend to be honest seamen, when really you are merciless pirates. As you approach the enemy ship, throw grappling hooks into their rigging and haul the two ships close together. Now you can swarm over their deck, fighting all the way.

false colours

We punish our enemies if they won't join us – or if we don't like the look of them. And we punish our own kind, if they betray us.

"If you are Lucky, we may leave you marooned on an island. If you're less Lucky, we'll throw you to the sharks!"

pirates boarding an enemy ship

A world at sea

It's an impressive sight, a fine ship with all its sails billowing in a stiff breeze. The helmsman turns the ship's wheel, which moves the great rudder. All over the ship, pirates are busy helping to keep the ship in order.

1

3

Sea turtle — a rare source of fresh food

A ship is the pirates' home for months

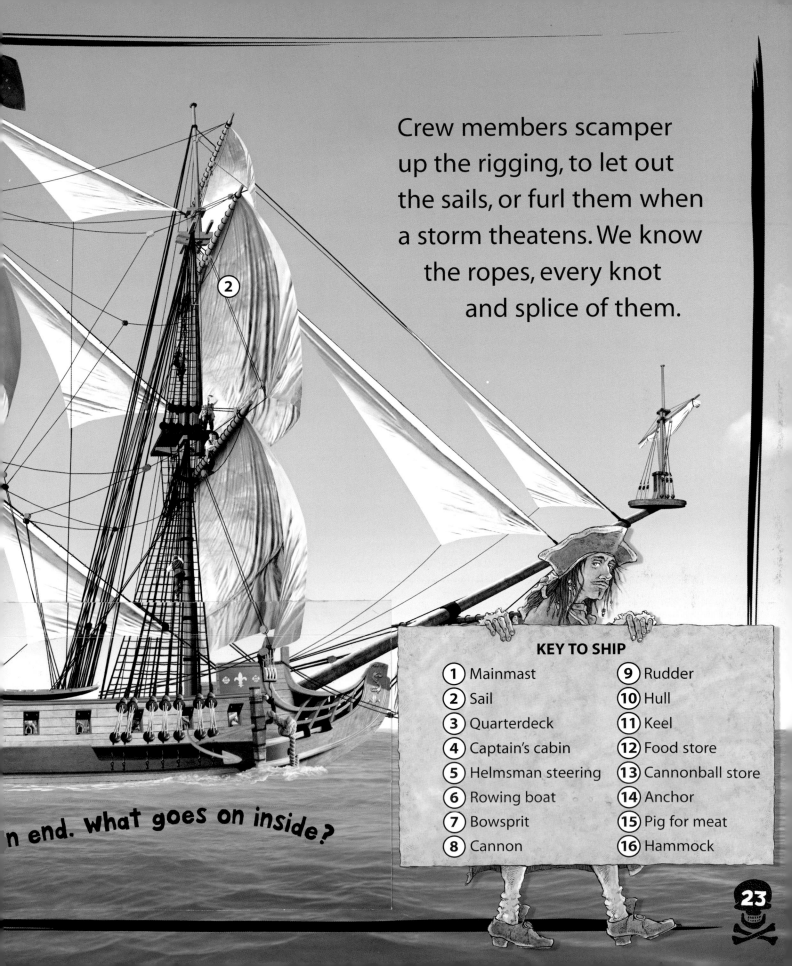

Crew members scamper up the rigging, to let out the sails, or furl them when a storm theatens. We know the ropes, every knot and splice of them.

n end. What goes on inside?

KEY TO SHIP

1. Mainmast
2. Sail
3. Quarterdeck
4. Captain's cabin
5. Helmsman steering
6. Rowing boat
7. Bowsprit
8. Cannon
9. Rudder
10. Hull
11. Keel
12. Food store
13. Cannonball store
14. Anchor
15. Pig for meat
16. Hammock

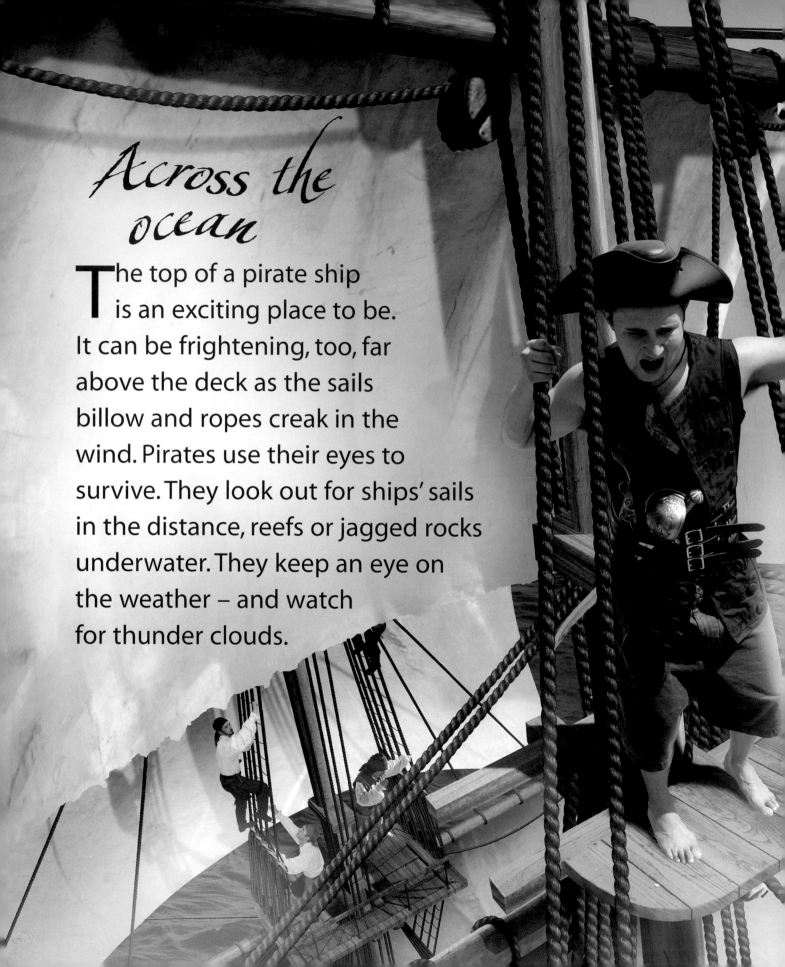

Across the ocean

The top of a pirate ship is an exciting place to be. It can be frightening, too, far above the deck as the sails billow and ropes creak in the wind. Pirates use their eyes to survive. They look out for ships' sails in the distance, reefs or jagged rocks underwater. They keep an eye on the weather – and watch for thunder clouds.

"Have you got a good head for heights? You'll need it up here on a breezy day!"

Clever pirates know all about charts and compasses, and those latitude lines on maps that help them find our position at sea. They can check their course against the sun and stars.

Ship's log

How did pirates know where they were?

Treasure!

Precious cargoes cross the seas, and all are there for the taking. Silks and spices, ivory and indigo, jewels and rum. Even anchors, ropes, medicines, cattle or maps can be sold for good money. And many a sea captain has a fine pair of pistols or a fancy ring on his finger. But most of all, pirates dream of gold…

Captain Kidd burying treasure (1690s)

Spanish gold doubloon

cutlass

rich silk cloth

powder horn

"Give me gold coins or any riches. I can share them with my shipmates or hide them away!"

pistol

jewels

gold plate and goblet

27

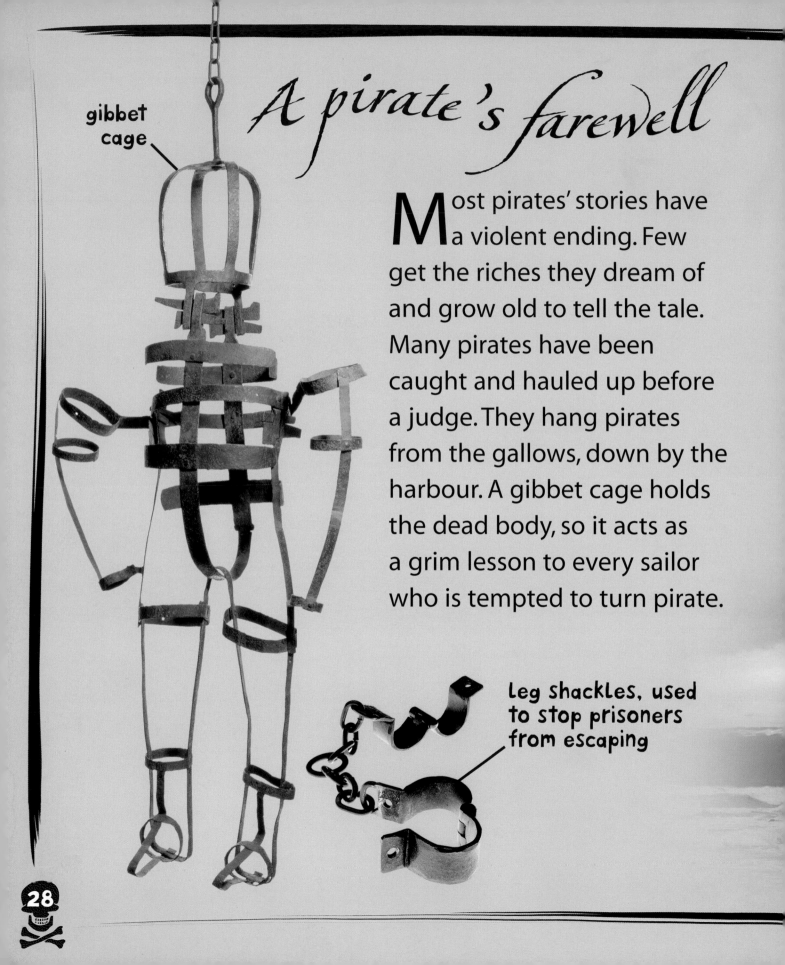

gibbet cage

A pirate's farewell

Most pirates' stories have a violent ending. Few get the riches they dream of and grow old to tell the tale. Many pirates have been caught and hauled up before a judge. They hang pirates from the gallows, down by the harbour. A gibbet cage holds the dead body, so it acts as a grim lesson to every sailor who is tempted to turn pirate.

Leg shackles, used to stop prisoners from escaping

I for one would rather die bravely in battle with my pistol in my hand, or be shipwrecked in a wild storm at sea.

Captain Kidd's trial in 1701

"Poor Jake or rich Jake, which shall it be? I might lose my new gold and jewels, but there's always more to be won!"

ship wrecked on a rocky shore

Glossary

anchor A heavy weight used to keep a ship still. It can be trailed in the water or stuck in the seabed.

buccaneers Pirates who fought in the Caribbean and Central America in the 1600s.

compass A magnetic instrument with a needle that always points north.

corsair A pirate, especially one that fought in the Mediterranean Sea in the 1500s, or a ship used by corsairs.

cutlass A short sword used by sailors and pirates.

grappling hook A metal hook thrown onto an enemy's ship, to pull it closer.

hold Where cargo is stored inside a ship.

hull The outer shell of a ship.

latitude A line marking distance north or south of the equator, which is an imaginary line that runs around the middle of the earth.

maroon To leave someone behind on a remote shore or island.

navigation Finding your way at sea.

Pirate Round A route between North America and the Indian Ocean, used by pirates from the 1670s onwards.

rigging Ropes that help to hold up a ship's masts and sails.

ship's log A book recording details of a ship's voyage.

sloop A light, fast sailing ship with a single mast.

splice To join together sections of split or frayed rope.

Index

Acknowledgements

The publisher would like to thank the following for permission to reproduce their material. Every care has been taken to trace copyright holders. However, if there have been unintentional omissions or failure to trace copyright holders, we apologize and will, if informed, endeavour to make corrections in any future edition.

Key: *b* = bottom, *c* = centre, *l* = left, *r* = right, *t* = top

4*bl* akg-images/Touchstone Pictures/Album; 5*tr* akg-images/Touchstone Pictures/Album; 5*br* Corbis/ Michael S. Yamashita; 7*tr* Corbis; 8*tr* Corbis/Araldo de Luca; 9*tr* The Art Archive/Historiska Muséet Stockholm/Dagli Orti; 9*bl* Corbis/Christie's Images; 9*br* Ancient Art & Architecture Collection Ltd; 12*tl* Topfoto/HIP/British Library; 12*tr* Mary Evans Picture Library; 13*tl* Getty Images/Hulton Archive; 13*tr* Topfoto/HIP/British Library; 19*tl* (Dutch cutlass), c.1771 © National Maritime Museum, London; 19*tl* (Pistol), Heritage-Images/Royal Armouries; 20*tr* Photolibrary Group Ltd./IndexStock; 22*bl* Getty Images/The Image Bank/Jeff Hunter; 26*bl* (gold doubloon), Corbis/Archivo Iconografico, S.A.; 26*tr* Topfoto; 28*l* The Bridgeman Art Library, Gibbet, c.1780 (wrought iron) by American School, (18th century) © Atwater Kent Museum of Philadelphia; 28*bc* Getty Images/Stone/ Tom Schierlitz; 29*tr* Alamy/Mary Evans Picture Library.

The publisher would like to thank the following illustrators:
Thomas Bayley 14–15, 16–17, 18–19, 21, 22–23, 24–25, 29; Sebastian Quigley 10–11, 26–27; Lyn Stone (Jake Rattlebones and incidentals throughout); Steve Weston 6–7, 8; Peter Winfield 13, 15, 19, 20.

The publisher would like to thank Kathleen McQuillan-Hoffman, and all at the Providence Maritime Heritage Foundation and the Continental Sloop Providence (www.sloopprovidenceri.org), for assistance with the book.